D0338833

THE IRREPRESSIBLE
CONFLICT

THE IRREPRESSIBLE CONFLICT

BUSINESS VS. FINANCE

BY

DAVID CUSHMAN COYLE

Select Bibliographies Reprint Series

BOOKS FOR LIBRARIES PRESS

FREEPORT, NEW YORK

STANDARD BOOK NUMBER:
8369-5148-4

LIBRARY OF CONGRESS CATALOG CARD NUMBER:
73-103648

PRINTED IN THE UNITED STATES OF AMERICA

PREFACE
To Third Edition

This book in its first two editions was so favorably received that it seems to be turning into a sort of periodical. So much of what appeared in the second edition as hopeful guessing must now be rewritten as history that for this edition the book has had to be done over from end to end. This time, I hope, the result is visionary enough so that a fair proportion of it will not have become history before Fall.

There are many possible roads to prosperity; as to which is the best or the most probable, deponent saith not. This is not a detailed plan for a new social order, but merely an essay in reorientation of thought. My acknowledgments are due to many men and women who by keen discussion—not always by complete agreement—have helped to hammer these ideas to a cutting edge: Dr. Virgil Jordan of *The National Industrial Conference Board*, Henry Saylor of *Architecture*, my sister Dr. Grace L. Coyle, H. S. Buttenheim of *The American City*, H. S. Braucher of the National Social Work Council, Dr. Alfred D. Flinn of the Engineering Foundation, Dr. Harlow Person of the Taylor Society, Dr. Henry Pratt Fairchild of New York University, R. E. Flanders of the American Engineering Council, Mr. Bernard Flexner, Dr. Luther Gulick of the Bureau of Municipal Research, Prof. Felix Frankfurter of Harvard Law School, John Hogan of the American Society of Civil Engineers, Dr. Ernest Minor Patterson and Prof. E. H. Welch of the Wharton School of the University of Pennsylvania, John Nolen and Norman T. Newton of the American Society of Landscape Architects, Kenneth Reid of *Pencil Points*, John Carmody of McGraw Hill Co., Morris Llewellyn Cooke, and many others whose keenness, courage, and vitality give grounds for faith in the future.

It is only fair to say that the economic principles herein set forth are old stuff; they go back to Hobson, and even to Malthus and Lord Lauderdale over a century ago. Their works were gathering dust on the shelves while we rushed toward our fate; but now the time is ripe, the crisis is upon us, the hiss of collapsing shirt-fronts is all about us; we must play up now or give way to those who will. This little book is one vote in favor of playing up.

D.C.C.

New York, June 1, 1933.

Preface to Fourth Edition

The world do move.

D.C.C.

Washington, Dec. 27, 1933.

THE IRREPRESSIBLE CONFLICT

BUSINESS VS. FINANCE

During the past few years our economic system has been in the condition of the centipede that lay distracted in the ditch considering how to run. We had the makings of a high standard of living, but we were paralyzed as if by some strange insanity. As a matter of fact, all that is really the matter with us is that our past history has left us with a set of ideas that no longer fit the facts.

When the United States was finally established after the Revolution, the new nation found itself in serious financial straits. The currency was hopeless, the public debt was worth about ten cents on the dollar, we owed large sums abroad, and our manufacturing equipment was inadequate. It was time to pull in the belt and build up the country. Frugality and hard work held the only hope of survival. Hamilton's policies—full payment of the depreciated state bonds and a protective tariff—were sound economics. They diverted money from consumers who might have spent it on their own pleasures, to financiers who would use it to build factories, and later to develop railroads and great cities. If sometimes speculation ran to excess and hard times came, the population continued to increase, so that in a few years the market caught up with the price of land and the equipment of industry, and the advance was resumed.

It is natural that after a hundred and forty years of that sort of growth, we should believe in the virtues of thrift and hard work, and in the automatic return of prosperity, after hard times, by the action of natural forces. A large part of our dismay in the past two years has been due to the apparent conflict between virtue and results, and to a growing fear that the healing forces of nature might have lost their power. Before we can hope for a workable adjustment to the conditions of modern industry, it is vitally necessary to clear up this apparent discrepancy between the facts and what we had always thought was economic law.

The world of 1790 has passed into history and has been replaced by a very different one. The machine age, with its enormous demands for capital and labor, was then still in its infancy. Now we are at the threshold of the power age, and the insistent demand is not for labor, not for capital, but for buyers to carry away the goods.

In the power age there are two new mechanical factors. One is that electric power has made it possible to start and stop each machine in a factory independently by throwing a switch. The other is that the electric eye, the thermostat, and other instruments of the sort, have been developed to take the place of the human machine tender. From these inventions has grown a new conception, the automatic factory, where both the physical labor and the routine machine tending are done by non-human agencies. A few skilled mechanics and engineers are the only human beings about the shop.* As the automatic factory spreads from one industry to another, labor is being abolished as a factor in production. This is the "technological revolution" now well under way. The statistics indicate that after 1923, although there was a considerable growth of output, the labor employed in manufacturing actually decreased.† Industrial efficiency had finally begun to

---

*See Walter N. Polakov: *The Power Age*, 1933.

†See F. C. Mills: *Economic Tendencies in the United States*, National Bureau of Economic Research, 1932. p.290.

discharge men in good times faster than industrial growth could make places for them; technological unemployment had become a present fact. Evidently there must be some new adjustment by which those who cannot be employed in making or distributing goods may yet be enabled to buy their necessary share of the product.

Still another feature of the power age seems to be developing. An automatic factory, with all its expensive instruments, may be more productive than an old fashioned plant of equal cost and much larger size. No statistics are yet available to prove this possibility, but the most competent engineers believe that some such relation will appear in many industries as the power age develops. The implications are far reaching. If a million dollars invested in new plant can force the abandonment of more than a million dollars worth of existing plant, the time may come when the total capital investment of the country will diminish as industry grows, instead of increasing as it did all through the machine age. The fact that at the moment there is an excessive amount of old plant still on hand is, of course, an additional reason for expecting a high death rate of capital for some time to come.

Apparently the power age is going to have comparatively little use for either labor or capital. Thrift and hard work, our ancestral virtues, are drugs on the market. The power age requires something quite different. It requires raw materials, power, and technical brains, all of which we have in abundance. It requires markets, and there, for the moment, is where we are stuck.

The power age, evidently, will demand an economic structure so adjusted that income will be distributed to people who have no connection with the production of goods, and that income will be allocated almost entirely to spending and hardly at all to the accumulation of new capital. The approach of the day when these adjustments would have to be made has been heralded, throughout the last thirty years, by a number of progressive changes, all of which tend to make the old machine-age adjustments unworkable.

Signs of Coming Change

During the War the United States lost its foreign debts, and in their place was erected a mountain of foreign credit that effectively makes impossible the "favorable balance of trade." On balance, from now on, there can be no net foreign market for our excess production. On the contrary, if we want our interest paid by our foreign debtors, we must consume more than we produce. It is therefore futile to look to the recovery of foreign markets to take up the slack in our own. It is they who must look to us to pull them out of the hole by our accepting their surplus products in payment of their obligations. The United States is accordingly forced to take the lead in meeting the new conditions. The events of 1933 are a detailed commentary on that fact.

Another change is the slackening of the growth of population, which in this country is evidently approaching a maximum. Depressions can no longer cure themselves automatically by the simple effect of an increase in the number of consumers. From now on, if the market for goods is to grow up to the present capacity of productive plant, it can do so only by the increase of average buying power, not by the arrival of more buyers. A general rise in the standard of living has now become the only possible outlet for a rising tide of goods for sale.

These two developments have accentuated the effect of the technological revolution, making increasingly imperative that some new method of distributing buying power be brought into play. Then, too, there have been several disquieting changes in the behavior of the business cycle.

INCREASED VIOLENCE OF THE BUSINESS CYCLE

As industry becomes more mechanized it becomes more unstable. Fixed charges are high compared with the labor item. Profits are large when the market is good; but when the market falls off the effect is disastrous. Retrenchment in the labor item requires drastic cuts; buying power collapses violently; and the market goes into a tailspin, wrecking the capital structure as well. The result is that the business cycle tends to become more stormy as mechanization proceeds.

Another development also has come to aggravate the instability of the market. As the country has become more productive a larger part of its product has come to be made up of durable goods like automobiles, electric refrigerators, and houses. Durable goods are bought freely in good times; but when hard times threaten, the old car and the old house have to do until times improve. The result is that the market collapses and times get worse instead of improving.

The most serious development, however, has been in the behavior of the capital markets. As the national income increased a larger and larger proportion of it went into investment. The idea that the boom years were years of extravagance is an optical illusion. They were years of thrift. At the peak, nearly a seventh of the national income was being invested each year.

When money is invested it is returned to circulation and reappears in the buying market as wages in the construction and machinery industries. But there is a secondary effect that is not so beneficial. Bonds feel very pleasant in the bank box, but in the balance sheet of the corporation they appear as liabilities. If too much money is invested in bonds, business at last finds itself with too many liabilities, and a depression sets in, during which some of the bonds are defaulted. This is called a "wholesome scaling down of values" by those who happen to be out from under. It is indeed a normal and necessary process, though painful. The business cycle has been made up largely of alternating periods of overinvestment and removal of the excess capital by bankruptcy.

In each depression the "corner" beyond which came revival was the place where enough bankruptcies had occurred to wipe out enough business debts so that there was room for a wave of new investment and new debt-building. But with all the trends pointing toward greater violence of the business cycle, sooner or later the downswing was bound to smash through the limit of emotional endurance. In fact, in 1932, when we saw the amount of bankruptcy we had to swallow this time in order to clear the way for revival, we could not bear to go through with it. The R. F. C. and the Federal Reserve were called upon to stop the wave of bankruptcy. The "corner" was too hot to pass.

The End of an Era may be defined as the moment when the customary adjustments become too painful to be endured, and something new has to be tried. The United States came to that moment in 1932, and 1933 is being devoted to a vigorous effort to set up new adjustments under governmental auspices. When successful readjustments are established in course of time, they will necessarily be oriented to the two fundamental requirements of the power age: an adequate

distribution of income to all our people; and a proper
allocation of the national income between investment
and spending.

New Adjustments to the Power Age

The central economic law of the power age is that
business cannot stand too much capital. Surplus
capital means surplus overhead, and if more capital is
injected into business than it can carry the excess has
to fall out again in bankruptcies and unbalanced bud-
gets. It is evident that the moral precepts of Benjamin
Franklin do not fit the necessities of times like these.
From now on, the intolerable sin is not extravagance
but avarice.

The material manifestation of the law that business
cannot stand excessive thrift is the overequipment of
industry. When too much money is poured into the
securities markets, office buildings and factories and
oil wells are enthusiastically started on all sides. Then,
while they are under construction, buying power is
high and business seems to be sound. But it is an unhealthy stimulant that is intoxicating business; for the
very source of this purchasing power lies in the construction of new competition and new debt. When the
new oil wells are brought in, and the new office buildings are ready to steal each other's tenants, suddenly
the overhead begins to swallow up the profits. Business
has been poisoned by the overexpansion of its means of
production—by too much thrift. Too many dollars
that should have been spent on opera tickets have been
invested in unnecessary mills and unrentable floor
space. "The very large investment which took place in
most countries in the years preceding 1929 has created a
surplus capacity almost everywhere, and ·   not clear

in what directions investment should be made in the near future."*

Justice Brandeis, in a dissenting opinion in 1932,† expressed the emergence of this new principle, as well as the dilemma that results from it. He says: "Some thoughtful men of wide business experience insist that all projects for stabilization and proration must prove futile unless, in some way, the equivalent of the certificate of public convenience and necessity is made a prerequisite to embarking new capital in an industry in which the capacity already exceeds the production schedules. . . . The objections to the proposal are obvious and grave. . . . Each of the thousands of judgments involved in carrying out the plan would call for some measure of prophecy. . . . Man is weak and his judgment is fallible."

The law in the New State Ice Co. case was a crude attempt to plan the allocation of capital. The secondary effects of this plan would not, however, be cumulative. Capital, forbidden to enter one industry, would look elsewhere for investment, so that if any industry were not already sick, it would soon be made so. If the law could be established for the whole country, capital would be forced into foreign bonds. Foreign bonds, as we now know, are a promise on our part either to find a market in this country for an immense excess of imports, or to submit to repudiation. The law, then, would merely transfer the poisonous effects of excess capital from one place to another. Furthermore, the possibilities of wrong judgment and undue influence are, as Justice Brandeis says, enough to make the success of such a measure very doubtful.

---

*League of Nations Report: *The Course and Phases of the World Economic Depression*, September, 1931.

†New State Ice Co. v. Ernest A. Liebman.

All these objections apply to any scheme for allocation of capital, particularly where no power is given to "allocate" the capital right away from any form of investment whatever.

ECONOMIC PLANNING

Planning is evidently going to be necessary to make the power age work, but the Ice case illustrates the fact that simply planning the first thing that comes to hand is not the answer. A plan, to do any good, must be more than a mere alleviation of some uncomfortable situation. For one thing, the secondary effects must not counteract the primary effect. Bootstraps plans that automatically cancel themselves make up 62% of economic literature. Moreover, no plan can be successful if it demands more prophetic genius than the human race can supply. Forecasters have acquired a remarkably black eye of late years. Finally any plan that takes a hero to work it and a well-disciplined people to carry it out is a poor bet for the long pull. While the hero stays in the White House and the people are sufficiently scared by the emergency to obey orders, marvels of organization can be carried through; but for the long pull, adjustments will need to be found that are not too bright and good for human nature's daily food.

There is always the danger, especially in ordinary dull times, that those who are appointed to plan the national effort may turn out to be mere factfinders. The temptation to resort to factfinding as an escape from the demand for action, and the temptation to resort to gestural action as a means of avoiding the inevitable, are both common to our well-known human nature, especially when its feet have grown used to the

comfortable desks of power. The most essential of all
plans, therefore, is a plan for reducing the necessary
scope of national planning within the possible range of
human capacity.

For example, six months' experience of the N. R. A.
indicates that parts of it may be within the range of
practical possibility, while other parts are likely later
on to lead into impassable quagmires. Moderate limita-
tion of hours and a low minimum wage can perhaps be
established and maintained. A few standards of fair
practice can probably be agreed upon and enforced.
But when we come to production and price control,
experience indicates that the chance of satisfactory
results is small. Production control, by merger or
cartel or trade agreement, is one of those ideas that
sound all right in theory but fail to work in practice.
When the market falls off the price is pegged by con-
trolling the output, which means, in plain English,
going on short time at the expense of the employees.
So all the uncartelized producers, such as farmers, find
that their customers have had their incomes reduced;
and the price of farm products tumbles heavily, reducing the purchasing power of the farmers. All the deflation is thus temporarily concentrated in consumers'
incomes, i. e., in the only source of business, with the
result that the last state of industry is worse than the
first. The effect of cartels in aggravating business instability was emphasized in the League of Nations
Report on the depression, previously quoted. This
type of device, then, is not a sound method of pro-
moting stability, because its secondary effects are fatal
to stability.

Another difficulty with production control is that it
leads naturally to a quota system, which practically
guarantees to all existing companies the right to live,—

as if we should abolish natural death among human beings. We sometimes forget that among the greatest benefits of an inscrutable Providence is the fact that we do not have to plan who among us shall die and when. The Government that abolishes natural death among industries may find that being the Lord God is no bed of roses.

The instability that results from allowing any part of the economic system to peg its prices at the expense of the remainder finally forces the unorganized parts of the system into similar methods of control. Thus the effect of industrial mergers in this country has been to compel the control of farm production. If this evolution were to continue beyond the emergency the outcome would be quite different from the price-pegging system from which it started. The situation would require a general staff with power, which would control all production in the interest of stability. It is obvious that it could not work like a cartel, for a cartel is a device for trying to shift the losses to somebody else, and there would be nobody else. The general staff could not restrict its payroll, since that would directly cut off its market. Profits could not be allowed to accumulate beyond the needs of normal growth, because their expenditure is vitally needed to keep up the market*, and they could not be distributed by paying them out on extension of plant, because that would pyramid the overhead. In order to operate, then, such a system would have to fix prices, wages, and incomes to keep consumption up to production, which makes it technically indistinguishable from the communist state. Italy is now progressing in this direction with considerable speed. The question still remains, however, whether the necessary forecasting ability could be'

*Henry Pratt Fairchild: *Profits or Prosperity?* Harpers, 1932.

mustered in the general staff to plan successfully the whole productive effort of so complex a nation as ours, or the necessary courage and power to make us obey its decisions. Our people have been selected from all the nations of the earth for their cleverness in avoiding obedience to arbitrary authority. It is questionable whether the American people are temperamentally suited to militarized planning, and whether we could easily find rulers with enough vitality to stand up to us after the crisis is past.

Even the American people will, however, accept and obey laws that are forced upon them by the pressure of circumstances. Two kinds of production planning are evidently unavoidable. One is the control and allocation of limited and irreplaceable natural resources. Any sort of economic system that will let the engineers produce what they can produce will soon run up against the limits of certain raw materials, and then conservation will cease to be questionable by anybody. The other field for production planning is in the industries that naturally tend to become monopolies, such as power, communication, transportation, and some others —a list that will perhaps grow with time. An important characteristic of this list is its comparative freedom from uncontrollable instability. Those industries in which capricious changes are least to be feared offer the best field for such meagre prophetic powers as are likely to be within the reach of a Governing Board.

The great majority of American industries and occupations, however, are evidently destined for decentralization. Many influences will push in this direction, as the progressive discrediting of investment bankers gradually frees industry from the irrational control of finance. Cheap power, good roads, the chance to do without stuffed shirts and high priced conferences, the advantages of local markets and personal management, all tend to the ultimate advantage of the small independent unit. An area having many small industries is naturally stable, and requires no detailed planning from Washington. The most important phase of national planning of industry, therefore, will be the development of means for encouraging decentralization. The most practical of all industrial plans are plans for making detailed plans unnecessary.

PUMPING MONEY INTO BUSINESS

These, however, are side issues. The essential adjustments are concerned with the distribution of income and the allocation of income between equipment and comsumption.

The master plan of the economic system for a power age will necessarily be a plan for directing the flow of money. All other plans are either supplementary to this central objective or else inconsequential.

The traditional method of directing the flow of money from one part of the economic system to another is by use of the tax system. Taxes are the most powerful pump we know of. The protective tariff, set up to pump money into manufacturing, did the job, despite leaks and protests. In spite of graft and evasion and politics, the most successful attempts of an unruly people to direct its own line of development have been made by the use of the tax laws. We have done it before; let us see whether there is a possibility of doing it again.

The present problem is how to divert money from investment in commercial equipment to the consumption of the goods that business is trying to sell. Whatever the ostensible point on which the tax is laid, the only thing that is of practical consequence is who really pays it and what effect does that have on his behavior. Taxes on trade, such as tariffs, sales, excise, and nuisance taxes, are "passed on" to the consumer. Most municipal taxes, laid on real estate, are either directly paid by that same consumer or passed on to him in higher costs. Whereupon the business man rubs his hands and thinks he has done something, forgetting that his only source of income is the consumer's pocket. Every chamber of commerce ought to print on its letterhead: "Costs passed to the consumer are passed to the business man who depends on him for a living." When it comes to correcting the maladjustment between saving and spending a different kind of tax is needed.

The taxes which draw from money headed toward investment are the higher brackets of the personal income and inheritance levies. The effect of these taxes is passed on not to the consumer, but to the promoter and the bond house. The heavier these taxes are made, the less money there will be for investment in the over-equipment of industry.* For the sake of argument, consider the effect that would be produced by the establishment of a "ceiling" of personal income. Above this ceiling the supertax would take practically all the surplus income, except as the taxpayer could show that he had contributed it to some project of a non-commercial kind. The percentage of exempt contributions could be limited to suit the need of funds for public works.

The immediate effect of such a tax would of course be that which business is seeking. Large sums which in good times would normally be reinvested in poison would be diverted to building art museums and hos-

*See Andrew W. Mellon: *Taxation: The People's Business*, Macmillan Co., 1924, pp. 12,18, 20, 122.

pitals and college libraries. Whether any particular
project were wisely conceived and economically carried out would be a problem for the sociologist and for
the technicians immediately concerned. So far as the
business man is interested as a business man, all that
matters is that it should not compete with business.
Money would be spent, there would be profits to be
made and workmen spending their wages in the stores;
and at the end of the job no new competitors to fear.

Public Spending

The function of public and semipublic spending has
been widely misunderstood. One of the universal
characteristics of American life is that a committee can
always be formed to raise money and do something for
the community. In normal times there is also a con-
tinual growth in governmental spending, as the desires
of the people find expression in new public services.
There is no danger of a lack of specific plans for spending money on cultural expansion.

There is danger of confusion about how to pay for all
these improvements. One principle the pressure of
events will inevitably enforce—that the source of funds
for a spending program must be surplus income, not the
income that would be spent anyway. The idea that
self-liquidating public works pay for themselves is just
one of those thoughts that have helped to give the last
few years that fine nutty flavor. Self-liquidating public
works do not pay for themselves. Somebody pays for
them. The consumer, on whom business depends for a
living: he pays for them. He also pays the local taxes,
and the sales taxes, and the nuisance taxes; then he
spends what little he has left. Business gets no added
market by spending money that would have been spent

anyway. Bootstraps again. Prosperity is made and preserved by spending money that would otherwise be invested. Income tax money, or its equivalent.

The fact is that the true function of public "capital" plant such as bridges, parks, and public buildings is not to supply money income to the Government, but to supply free services to the people. So far, indeed, as the economic aspect of the matter goes, the real utility of an extensive public plant is that it serves as an instrument of stabilized public expenditure for personnel and maintenance. During this depression the maintenance of existing public operations was one of the few fairly stable sources of buying power in a collapsing world.

A second danger lies in the belief, now unfortunately widespread, that cutting down expenses makes the country richer. This idea, a relic of the preceding ages of scarcity, is no longer valid. When the production of wealth, material and non-material, is limited not by the power to produce but by the power to sell, then the spending of money makes the country richer and the failure to spend it makes the country poorer. The economic law of the age of plenty is that, within the limits of energy available to produce wealth, the total national income is just about equal to the total national expenditure, whatever the latter may be. A "deficit" appears whenever expenditure is so reduced that the income falls below the "fixed" or involuntary expenses. A "surplus" appears whenever the expenditure is increased until the income becomes much larger than the involuntary payments for interest, local taxes, food, and the like, leaving a margin for comforts and luxuries. The more is spent, the more people are at work, the more wealth is made, the more income there is. The way to abolish a deficit is to spend more, not less.

But since no individual dares to tackle his own deficit by spending enough to bring back prosperity, the Government has to act as general spender to lift the national income in depression and to support it in prosperity. That is the law of the age of plenty; and no permanent adjustment will be attained until it is obeyed. However luxurious the services which that kind of spending may provide for the people, it cannot justly be called extravagant. The more of this kind of spending there is, the more market there will be for business, the more men will be actively employed, and the more wealth will be created. The creation of wealth, whether it be shoes or education or just the widespread feeling of economic security, is surely not extravagance. If it is necessary that the Federal Government shall collect billions of dollars every year and spend them on beautifying the country, so that, as a by-product, mechanical industry may be running full time producing material wealth for the whole population to enjoy, then those billions are certainly money well spent.

Business, moreover, suffers not only from the debt burden and the competition caused by overinvestment, but also from the instability of the market due to technological unemployment. Something has to be done to furnish spending-money to the laborers displaced by machines, or else the product of the machines cannot be sold. The proposed tax will directly improve this condition. The supertax, whether spent by the Government or exempted and given to private philanthropy, will go mostly for services as distinct from manufactured goods. Now it is in the field of services, of work that does not require any significant amount of mechanical power and raw material, that the only potentially unlimited field for human labor exists. A very large expansion of this field is the only practical solution of the problem of employment for the men displaced by machines. The improvement of living conditions, of health, knowledge, and art, the beautification of city and country, modern methods of treatment for criminals and defectives, the elimination of agricultural pests, the provision of recreation facilities, and a host of other "cultural" or quasi-cultural improvements, with all the various grades of labor and management required, must be the field of occupation in future for most of our population. Already there is observable a tendency in this direction. The Business Week* reports that from 1919 to 1930 the market for goods increased about 12%, while the market for services, private and governmental, increased 50%. The proposed tax, by turning money into public or semi-public services, would accelerate this healthy trend in which lies the only practical cure for technological unemployment.

For although services are the answer, and the final answer, to technological unemployment, they have the disadvantage that they are naturally prone to disappear in depression. Deliberate stabilization of the service market is one of the most essential requirements of the new economic balance.

The secondary effects of the proposed tax would be cumulative. The point of diminishing returns would be far overpassed, and the result would be partially to dry up the sources of the tax, a result to be deplored as much as the drying up of a boil on the back of a man's neck. Some investment funds would be transferred to tax-exempt securities, reducing the volume of money pressing for investment, and making it possible to refund the government debt at a very low rate of inter-

*May 4, 1932.

est.* High incomes "from business or profession" could
not, of course, be transferred to tax-exempts in this
way, and would continue for some time to be a source
of public revenue, until the lack of incentive had led to
their partial elimination. A high inheritance and gift
tax would force the dissipation of the great fortunes
and partly counteract the effect of new savings by
actual liquidation of previously invested funds. The
incentive to accumulation beyond the ceiling level
would be greatly reduced, and this would discourage
the growth of new fortunes to take the place of the
old. (And will men of ability work if there is no chance
to become a millionaire? Look at the Church, and the
civic associations, and the college faculties, and the
scientific laboratories, and all the innumerable unpaid
officers of organizations. Energy is our middle name.)
The comparative scarcity of large fortunes would not
only be good for business, but would make their visi-
bility very high and simplify the problem of enforce-
ment. The generally high enforceability of income tax
laws, even under adverse conditions, was illustrated in
the case of Al Capone.

All these effects would tend to the elimination of the
dangerous concentrations of investing power, and their
dissipation into smaller units of income. As the percentage of income saved and invested is apt to be
roughly proportional to the size of the income, it is
evident that the total effect would be to decrease the
parsimony of the well-to-do. At the same time the
danger of industrial paralysis would be reduced, and a
smaller volume of savings would give a greater measure
of security to all classes.

Another secondary effect would be that some of the
owners of large fortunes would flee abroad, taking their

*See A. W. Mellon: *Taxation: The People's Business.* p. 13, 17.

money with them. If the law were properly drawn, the only way to go abroad and escape the tax would be to withdraw from participation in American investments. The fortune would have to be liquidated, allowing the investment of an equal volume of new savings without increasing the total debt load on industry. Then the dollars would have to be sold for foreign credit or its equivalent. The foreigners who bought the dollars would then be supplied with the means of purchasing American exports. The net effect of the whole transaction would be to remove a large sum of money from the investment market where it could do nothing but harm and add it to the export market where it could do nothing but good to business. That sort of thing is what business needs more than anything else.

The primary effects of this sort of taxation are, then, in the right direction, and the secondary effects reinforce the primary. Mathematically, therefore, the tax is sound. As Mr. Mellon* himself has said, it would discourage enterprise. The rotting mass of dead enterprises now clogging our morgues is sufficient evidence of the vital necessity of discouraging enterprise in boom times. We took the opposite course last time, and the event was unpleasant.

Fortunately, Mr. Roosevelt is aware of the danger of encouraging enterprise. In his radio address of May 7th, 1933, he said: "I do not want the people of this country to take the foolish course of letting this improvement come back on another speculative wave... the ruinous practice of increasing our crop output and our factory output in the hope that a kind Providence will find buyers at high prices. Such a course may bring

---

*Sir Arthur Salter blames Mr. Mellon specifically for aggravating the boom and collapse by reduction of income-tax rates. *Recovery*, p. 78. See also: Mellon: *Taxation: The People's Business*, p. 12.

us immediate and false prosperity, but it is the kind of
prosperity that will lead us into another tailspin."

One of the most important virtues of regulation by
tax is that it requires so little in the way of prophecy.
It is like pumping the excess water out of the hold of
a ship. Opinions may differ as to just how much will
have to be pumped, and as to how many gallons per
minute will come out of the pumps; but if there is too
much water in the hold it takes no prophet to see that
pumping will be a good thing to do. By the same
token, if fortunes are being made in business at any
particular time, it takes no superbrain to recognize that
they must be kept out of reinvestment or hard times
will surely come. The savings of the poorer classes
alone will be enough to overload business and bring on
an occasional sick spell; no great accuracy of predic-
tion is needed to see that if the large incomes are diverted to spending, it will postpone depression and
make it less violent when it comes.

Still another element of soundness is the comparatively moderate amount of courage required to operate
a tax law of this kind. If it is once thoroughly under-
stood by business men that the more drastic the income
tax the more customers they will have, the danger of
the tax being reduced in good times will be quite small.
The "ceiling" will locate itself at a point where the
political power of those who want it lower will balance
that of those who want it higher. The Secretary of the
Treasury, backed by business, will be able to hold
out against the financial group without the exercise of
superhuman courage and endurance. For the workers
and farmers will be on the same side of the argument
as the business man, and that is a new and extremely
powerful lineup.*

*See also: Franklin D. Roosevelt: *Looking Forward*. John Day Co., 1933,
pp. 104–5.

It is evident, then, that the simultaneous decrease of overequipment and increase of buying power, required by business to prevent fatal paralysis, can be obtained in considerable degree by the use of the income and inheritance taxes if they are made sufficiently drastic. The primary effect will be to transfer money directly from the investment market to the market for goods and services. Another primary effect of equal importance will be a vast increase in public and semi-public expenditure for services, utilizing the labor that is no longer required in industry. The secondary effect will be to destroy the unhealthy accumulations of unspent money that are partly responsible for our excessive saving and inadequate spending. The action of the tax will be automatic, it will work when times are good and sleep when times are bad, requiring no superhuman knowledge and prophetic power to know when to turn it off and on. The potential political power of the interests which will benefit by such a tax is so overwhelming that no superhuman courage will be required to administer it. It is therefore sound on all points.

The graduated income tax has been presented here as an illustration of the sort of plan that will meet the fundamental requirements of business in a system of high productivity such as our own. With the graduated income tax, or its equivalent, established as the back-bone of the new economic order, a number of supplementary plans will arrange themselves around it by natural affinity.

Taxes on new security issues, the new law requiring full disclosure of the facts about new issues of stocks and bonds, stock transfer taxes, perhaps even a graduated corporation tax on gross capitalization, are examples of valuable means for obstructing investment and staving off the inflation of debt.

There is also an important group of plans for distributing one of the most characteristic products of the power age: leisure. Leisure *with* income.

Three plans for distributing leisure are well past their infancy. One is the effective prohibition of child labor. The second is the reduction of the length of the working week, with Government support and help in whipping the recalcitrants into line. The third is a generous and all-embracing old age pension. This last is particularly valuable because it will not only create a class of buyers who have nothing to sell, but will also render unnecessary the pathetic and hopeless effort to save up for old age, and will encourage people of all ages to spend as they go.*

Insurance Against Depression

When we failed to turn the "corner", and the Government had to step in and apply artificial respiration to business, the old self-operating business cycle ended. That, however, does not mean that in the future business will simply lie passive in a baby carriage pushed along a level road by Uncle Sam. There will still be ups and downs on account of movements of the population, changes of style, variations of crops, new inventions and discoveries, and similar influences, many of them outside of human control. A considerable part of modern industry depends on technological processes that may be superseded at any moment. Accordingly, the influence of unpredictable change is increasing. Since no provision can be made to prevent unexpected catastrophes there is a growing necessity for adequate methods of insuring against the effects of unpredictable events.

*See John Willard Roberts: *Building Permanent Prosperity*, published by the author, 528 Munro Ave., Mamaroneck, N. Y. 1933.

One proposal for stabilizing business is the "timing" of public works, to make them come in hard times when they are most needed. The procedure is usually conceived in somewhat the following manner. When unemployment is widespread and municipalities are forced to find public work to help the situation, they issue bonds which are sold to investors. This is entitled "local self-help." The investors obtain money to pay for these bonds either by selling other securities or by drawing from the banks, which thereupon sell securities to maintain their liquidity. The securities markets sink to low levels, as they did in 1931, and the solvency of all sorts of business is endangered by forced liquidation and hoarding.

When business is prosperous and taxes are easily collected the other end of this same process again acts to produce an unsound condition. The bonds are paid off, and the bondholders find themselves with lump sums in their hands which they naturally feel constrained to invest at once. The effect is to cause a rise in the securities markets, and to encourage the banks to float new issues.* Conditions such as those of 1928 prevail, too much money gets into superfluous equipment, and the conditions of 1930–31–32 naturally follow. Here again in helping to create the inflation, the process of paying off bonds to private investors when times are booming must bear part of the blame.

It is evident that what we should have here would be a rhythmic contraction and expansion of credit, caused by an attempt to "time" the public works program; and that the financial operations would do as much harm on their end of the process as the timing of public work would do good on the other end. That is, this is pulling our bootstraps; we can plan long-range public works

*See Mellon: *Taxation: The People's Business.* p. 31.

programs till we are blue in the face; so long as they are financed in this way the net effect will be practically zero if not worse.

There is, however, another way to finance public works in depression. If Federal bonds are sold to the Federal Reserve so as to expand currency or credit, then no strain is placed on the markets. On the contrary, the injection of new money into the market for goods tends to stop the depression.

When good times return and a Federal surplus develops, the bonds are paid, and the credit or currency based upon them is destroyed. This is a deflationary action and tends to prevent the dangerous inflation of business that always threatens when times are good. If the usual inflation of business can be prevented, then the bankruptcy of superfluous plants will be spread along during good times instead of piling up and landing on the country all at once as it did last time. In good times it would pay the Government to discourage saving and investment by paying its debts in such a way as to deflate the securities market. A public works program financed in this manner would not be a bootstraps affair, because the expansion and contraction of currency or credit incident to the program would have a cumulative effect, by helping to counteract the fluctuation of business.

To summarize: the vital factor in the temporary financing of public work as a relief from unemployment is this: *All bonds issued in depression to be paid off in prosperity must be so issued that they are made the basis of an expansion of currency or credit, and so paid off that their cancellation is the basis of a contraction of currency or credit.*

The whole inflation question has been needlessly obfuscated by disregarding the fact that everything depends on what is inflated and who gets it. Federal inflation for public works increases buying power and improves business. If the program is adopted on a sufficient scale to restore prosperity the inflation will automatically cease, provided the tax structure is strong enough to throw the Federal budget promptly into a surplus. After the War, for example, the heavy Federal inflation by which the war was financed ceased as the budget ran into a surplus. If the Government is weak and unable to lay heavy taxes, the inflation will run away, as it did in certain countries after the War. Governmental inflation is controllable in a strong country.

The other kind of inflation is the private inflation of stocks and credit. In a bull market the price of stocks is marked up a hundred billion dollars, which is actually fiat buying power in the hands of the holders of stocks. Some of this new fiat buying power is used as collateral for loans of fiat bank credit by which new issues of bonds are floated and new debts are loaded on the business structure. Another portion is used for further inflation of the stock market itself. Still another portion is used for influencing public opinion in favor of the new era, and for obtaining political power. The next step is to reduce the income tax, suppress the feeble efforts of the Federal Reserve to control credit, and go joyfully shooting up into the stratosphere. That is what happened. This second type of inflation is popularly called "sound money," and history teaches us that it is always uncontrollable.

America need not look to Germany or to the French Revolution for a lesson in the effect of printing worthless paper. We do it here too. Only our weakness is not for paper money but for Peruvian bonds.

Another form of business stabilizer is unemployment insurance. The principle involved is again that the financing must be so arranged that it will not counteract the primary action, but reinforce it. If the funds, as they are raised, are put in the bank, or loaned on call, or invested in any way, they will help to inflate business, and when they are withdrawn for use in paying benefits, they will thereby help to deflate business. If the funds are handled in this way, therefore, the financing helps to create the very instability which the funds are aimed to relieve. On the other hand, if the funds are hoarded in currency, and paid out of the bank box when needed, the result will be to reinforce the primary effect of the insurance. For hoarding in good times and dehoarding in hard times helps to stabilize business, and to reduce the amount of unemployment that the funds will be called upon to relieve. The soundness of an unemployment insurance plan, therefore, is vitally dependent on the method of handling the funds. If they are temporarily invested and withdrawn when needed the total effect of the program will be little or nothing; if they are held in currency or its strict equivalent, the effect will be cumulative.

Both unemployment insurance and timed public works are still mostly on paper in this country, but there is another type of insurance against hard times that has already been widely used. This is the habit of laying up corporation surplus for the purpose of paying dividends when not currently earned. The Corporation Reserve is the grandfather and President of the Bootstraps Club. Here the fallacious notion that "money should be made to work" has had the most devastating effects on the business world, and no program for stabilizing business will be really effective until this notion has been swept away. The method of using surplus earnings to bring on ruin is to deposit them in the bank during the early stages of prosperity. The banker naturally lends the corporation's money to one of its competitors for expansion of capacity, which stimulates business and for a time shows no indication of the inevitable crash. As the bubble grows larger and more irridescent, the corporations turn their surplus funds loose in the call market. This is called preserving a liquid condition, and is considered a conservative policy. Then when the bubble bursts, the companies draw out their funds, wrecking the banks or calling loans on speculators as the case may be, and generally deflating everything in sight. Now, it is undoubtedly a good thing for stability to have dividends paid when they are not earned as well as when they are; but if the funds for these payments are to be manipulated in such a way as to produce the maximum possible dislocation of business, what's the use?

Even more conservative and respectable is the twin brother of the bootleg-money policy, known as "ploughing in" or "sound management." It consists of using the earnings of the company to overexpand its plant to such an extent that competitors will be forced to cut prices until the industry is ruined. The idea that every man and every company can grow indefinitely at everybody else's expense is the basis for many an ambitious program, which when added to others of its kind paralyses the whole economic organism.

There is no way to squirm out of it. If one company could plough in its surplus and if nobody else in the country were allowed to do the same, it might be sound economics. But if corporation surplus in general is made to work, it can work nothing but disaster. The only safe place for money that is laid up for hard times is in the sock. Business will always be painfully unstable until that hard lesson has been learned. It goes against everything we have always believed. But if our past ideas of sound economics are still sound, why are we in such a mess? Something is loose somewhere, and this idea that unlimited investment pays is it.

Some day there will have to be a prohibitive tax on all corporation profits that are not either distributed immediately in dividends or laid aside in currency.

Incidentally that tax will dissuade the holders of large incomes from incorporating themselves and paying themselves starvation "dividends" in order to avoid the personal income tax.

Still another possible way of compensating the fluctuations of business is provided by the postal savings banks. In these banks the savings of the poorer classes are placed in the hands of the Government for safekeeping. Here, again, is a sizeable sum of money laid up in good times to be drawn upon in hard times. It could be largely increased if the Post Office would do a bit of propaganda. If the Government will adopt a policy of holding these funds in cash in good times and depositing them in the banks only in hard times, a stabilizing effect will be produced. But if they are deposited in the commercial banks as fast as they are received, the effect is to make business more unstable. The beneficial results of a sound policy in regard to these funds would be so great that the Government could well afford to pay two per cent for the privilege of holding and manipulating this mass of money for the public good. This is just another instance of the fact that a little less parsimonious saving at the spigot would save a large amount of wasting at the bung.

CREDIT CONTROL

Credit control, given first place by many orthodox economists, comes logically only after the measures that have here been described. The inflation of bank

credit in good times, and its use for long term investment, naturally require a corresponding deflation in
hard times, and a forced liquidation leading to defaults
and bankruptcies. The banks help to intensify the
normal saving-investment-loss sequence.

As long as prosperity is allowed to be built on a
"sound money" or Wall Street inflation, the control of
bank credit is impracticable. A "sound money" inflation places so much power in the hands of the men
whose activities need to be controlled that when the
moment for stopping the inflation arrives they are
likely to be found in possession of the banks, the Treasury, and even the White House. That, it will be re-
called, is what happened.

IMPLICATIONS

It is obvious that adequate measures to distribute
income and to promote spending at the expense of investment will have far reaching implications. Some of
these implications are worth careful examination.

Any successful attempt at limiting overequipment
necessarily implies a certain vested right in existing
industry not to be disturbed. As Justice Brandeis says:
"doubt is being expressed whether it is economically
wise or morally right that men should be permitted to
add to the producing facilities of an industry which is
already suffering from overcapacity." And yet, if new
inventions may not be installed and given their chance
to bankrupt the old, what about progress? The principle involved can be illustrated by considering extreme
cases. If no new machinery is permitted except to re-
place machines that are worn out, obsolescence costs
will be at a minimum, but progress will be slow and the
total net efficiency of the system will be low. On the

other hand, suppose that overcapacity were prevented
by constantly scrapping large quantities of equipment,
paying the costs out of a tax on business. This would
prevent the poison of idle machinery, but it would involve devoting most of the energies of the people to
setting up and taking down equipment. That is, progress would be fast but obsolescence costs would be
excessive and the overall efficiency would again be low.

Somewhere between these two extremes lies the
maximum overall efficiency, i. e., the maximum "real
income" in goods and services for all concerned. It will
be most nearly approached if the machinery of production is kept so scanty in amount that it will work the
maximum practicable number of shifts and wear out
as fast as possible before some new invention renders
it obsolete. The optimum rate of progress will be where
the costs of production, including not only the capital
charges for new machinery, but also the costs of elimi-
nating the old, and placing the displaced men, add up
to a minimum. Progress, then, has a limited optimum
rate of speed, and the vested right of existing plant not
to be disturbed is merely the right of business not to be
forced to progress too fast. Excessive progress means
an excessive scrapping cost and /or an excessive amount
of idle plant. For that reason, if we cut down overequipment and obsolescence, the process must involve
slowing the rate of progress to more nearly its optimum
figure.

The characteristic feature of a plenty economy is
that progress has reached a point where its natural rate
of speed is far above the optimum, and unless it is
artificially controlled the system stalls. As saving and
investment are what make progress, it follows that the
control of overinvestment is the key to the smooth op-
eration of business. The fact that progress has a lim-

ited optimum rate leads inevitably to the fact that the total opportunity for sound investment of savings is limited. The more money is diverted from investment to consumption, the more chance there is for the remaining capital to find sound investment. But if too much money gets into investment, then it all becomes unsound. It is like the capacity of a man's stomach, which is elastic but limited. The more he spends on golf and hunting trips, the more food he can get away with; but if he puts too much of his income into unnecessary food it will only make him sick. From this fact there follow certain important implications. Public policy demands that the savings of the poor be secure, because in hard times these savings are the first line of defence against destitution, doles, communist propaganda, and many other painful and dangerous effects. Now, if the total chance for sound investment is limited in amount, and if public safety requires the soundness of small savings, it follows that the right to invest money at will, instead of spending it, cannot remain free to all. Human laws and liberties have to adapt themselves to inescapable facts, and this is one of them. The investment of money is affected with a public interest on both ends. Not only must business have the right to veto its injection into overbloated industry, but the State must assert the right to assure itself that its poorer citizens get the first chance at what opportunities there are. *Neither Business nor the State dare tolerate reckless saving by those who have no need to save.*

The fact that the total value of all the investments in the country is limited and may even decrease in the future will necessarily have far reaching effects on life insurance reserves, foundations, endowments, and similar capital structures. In general there will evidently be a trend toward the use of current income from

premiums, or gifts as the case may be, in place of income
from capital for the functions now performed by these
agencies. Life insurance in particular may have to be
rearranged with a central reinsurance body, perhaps
even run by the Government with a reserve of paper
money to cover the net annual fluctuations of income
and outgo. The "cash value" would naturally become
extinct, and probably likewise the lump sum death payment. These changes are not recommended here as a
"plan;" they are suggested as a possible outcome of in-
exorable developments in the economic environment.

The function of wealth, under these conditions, is
very different from its function in the machine age now
closing. The millionaire as capitalist, collecting and
investing large sums of capital money, has become
obsolete. The millionaire in the role of Renaissance
prince, collecting large sums and spending them on
great cultural projects, is the type adapted to the age
of plenty. The high-bracket taxes, if they are properly
buttered with exemptions, will naturally set up a selec-
tive evolution. Millionaires of the now obsolete ac-
cumulative type may be expected to become gradually
extinct, leaving as survivors those whose idea of the use of
money is to build college dormitories or kill hookworms.

BUSINESS vs. FINANCE

It is evident that in attempting to free itself of the
poison of oversaving business is pulling the beard of
that man-eating ogre Finance.* It is only beginning to
be dimly recognized that in an age of plenty there is
and must be between the interests of business and those

---

*A high official of the late Administration, in a personal letter, criticized this
whole argument on the ground that any such action would "upset the financial
machine." Quite so. See: Louis D. Brandeis: *Other People's Money*, N. Y.,
Frederick A. Stokes Co., 1932.

of finance an irrepressible conflict. The normal processes of finance are poisonous to business. Finance causes instability. One way to make financial profits is to wait till business starts to be profitable, and then lend money to someone to set up a competing plant. Then when everybody naturally goes bankrupt, the lender gets the property, and if recovery ever does take place he is in on the ground floor. Business pays the cost. Another way is to buy securities when they threaten to go up, and hold them so that they will go up, and sell them when they threaten to go down, and sell short so as to help them go down. Business pays the cost. A third way to get financial profits is to set up an investment trust or a holding company that is so complicated that the small investor cannot see just how he is to be rooked. When his investment is gone, he becomes a poor customer for legitimate business. A fourth way is to take a commission from a foreign government for selling bonds to people who ask their banker for disinterested advice.* Still another way is to set up a merger, pass around slices of watered stock to influential friends and relatives, and then persuade the public to buy the stock for real money. In any case, business pays the costs either in rising overhead or falling sales or both. Business needs stability to prosper; finance gets its profits from instability. To be more specific: the income tax makes for stability and hurts finance; the sales tax makes for instability and hurts business. Over this conflict of interest there must be a battle, because so long as finance dominates business both are headed for the precipice, and finance will not loose its grip without a fight. The question whether they go over the edge together, either in this depression or in the next one, will be settled by whether

*See Salter: *Recovery*, p. 116–8.

business has the vitality to rouse itself and muster the power to reduce finance to its proper place as the servant of production. The crossroads of history will be the place where we do or do not develop means for keeping money out of Wall Street and making it travel up and down Main Street where it belongs.

THE SECURITIES MARKETS

The conflict between the interests of business and finance illuminates another important fact, the true relation between the securities markets and business.

If money is deliberately diverted from investment to spending in adequate amounts to keep overbuilding within bounds, it will cause low prices for stocks and bonds. The prosperity of trade due to active buying of goods and services will be accompanied by a low state of the stock market owing to scarcity of funds available for investment. The principle needs to be taught in all the schools, that sound business growth is marked *not* by rising securities markets, but by high rates of return on invested money. Sound business, whether in a surplus economy or in a new country, is business constantly straining to catch up with the demands of the market, not business desperately trying to dispose of its products; and sound business is therefore marked by high profits and high rates of return on its capital. If securities are paying high rates of return, it means that finance is calling for money and cannot get it, which means that machinery is going on double shifts and that extensions of plant are blocked for want of capital, which means that new debts and new competition are not being built up, which means that business is sound. But the "good times" that we have been accustomed to see are marked by rising stock markets, which means that new plant is being floated, which means that overhead is going to rise, which means that finance is already digging the hole for business to fall into. It is this sort of good times that the Federal Reserve was trying to bring on in 1932 by open market operations designed to raise the bond market. "Sound" opinion favored a movement to bring back good times by modernizing industrial plants all over the country; i. e., by preparing the means of intensified competition. That is a young one of the snake that bit us before.

It will be a new era when we see business active and prosperous without an inflation of the securities markets. When that happens it will be a fairly good sign that business has finance under control, after which eternal vigilance is the price of safety.

The Strategic Situation

It is one thing to say that there ought to be a law, and quite another to muster the power to get it and use it. Where can the power be found to clip the claws of the financial lion?

The first factor of power is economic interest. The diversion of money from capital overinvestment to consumption of goods and services is vitally necessary to industry and commerce, to the professions, to labor and the farmers. Producers, technicians, distributors, consumers—that is an extremely powerful preponderance of interest. On the other side stands uncontrolled finance, entrenched in power and with the prestige of history behind it. Finance has the whip hand, but if the true interest of all parties can be made clear, the situation is loaded for a shift of the center of power.*

---

*These sentences, from a previous edition, have been retained as a picture of the pious hopes of 1932. Since then the heavy artillery has come into action. Who has the edge now? Time will tell.

If the recent happenings in Washington are examined in the light of these facts it will be apparent that this is the very conflict which has been there struggling to find expression.

The second dynamic factor lies in the emotional desires of the people. Among our people dynamic emotion attaches to the idea of freedom of initiative. As has been pointed out, the communist solution, while mathematically sound, is seriously handicapped, for us, by our temperamental distaste for discipline. Capitalism as it has been organized also subjects the majority of our people to a galling yoke, and it is a vital fact that the measures which are necessary to save business will lead toward a wider spread of individual liberty. Great sums must be removed from the hands of financiers and put into the hands of buyers. That means not only more freedom of action for the buyers, but a measure of emancipation for business-men from the clutches of the banks. The necessary measures will remove the incentive of purely financial mergers, and the incentive to try to grow rich beyond all bounds. That means more chances for middle-sized concerns to survive, and therefore more openings for individual initiative and leadership. (For the restriction of available capital leads to a smaller total of equipment, not to a smaller number of companies operating it.) The necessary measures call for pouring money into the consumption of goods and services, which means not only more profitable business, but a relative scarcity of labor, and therefore more freedom for the laboring man. It appears, then, that business, in going up against the giant Finance, has the strategic advantage that what it is fighting for is what the American people want.

A third factor of power is to be in line with tides of evolution that are already beginning to flow. Such an evolutionary tide is the decentralization of industry from other causes than those that may come into action as an incident of the solution of the overinvestment problem. Crosby Field, of the American Society of Mechanical Engineers, has made an able study of the advantages of small industries.* John C. Cresswell in the Magazine of Wall Street† has noted the fact that in this depression small industries and regions dependent on small industries have survived better on the average than those in which ownership or management are heavily centralized. He says: "It is not impossible that we are now witnessing the obsolescence of business bigness in a great many fields. Perhaps it will remain only in those fields where it is clearly superior to little business, and will entirely withdraw from that twilight zone into which it has expanded only from a mania for greatness and a lust of power." It is an important strategic advantage that the necessary measures to free business from poison are in line with existing evolutionary trends.

A fourth factor of power is to have an adequate means of educating the public. Finance is notoriously close to the great sources of public information. But the White House is closer. The President can say what he thinks the people should hear, and he can be heard. So long as the White House is occupied by a man who is determined to bring before the public whatever measures may be required to make the economic system work, the chances of an improvement in public understanding of the situation are excellent. If the luck holds, and public opinion can be steered quickly enough to avoid

---

*Management of the Small Plant, Its Characteristics and Advantages. A.S. M.E., June 9, 1930.
†March 5, 1932.

disaster, the prospects of coming through into smooth water seem to be improving.

DAWN OF CIVILIZATION

This essay has dealt, from the engineer's standpoint, with relations that must necessarily exist between power production and the economic system. Even the emotional elements entangled in the economic order have been treated as natural unthinking forces exerting a measurable influence on the behavior of the whole system. Some such adjustments as have been here described are mechanically necessary to make the machine operate. To attain these adjustments business, with the help of Government, has to conquer finance and reduce it to subjection. But that is not the whole picture.

Even in the most difficult circumstances man is more than bread and clothes. In the age of plenty that now lies before us the economic process will not be the central feature of the social system, but only its service of supply. It is true that business and industry must be given enough attention to keep them in good running order; but once that is done the major interests of life will lie elsewhere.* When water comes unfailingly from a faucet it takes less daily care and attention than when it has to be carried from a well; and when all the material things can be easily come by they will fade into the background just as the modern conveniences do in any well regulated house.

Accordingly, the "planned economy" of the future must be regarded not as a system of rigid discipline and regimentation, but as a situation in which freedom will be greatly extended. Just as the automobile requires traffic laws but extends freedom of travel, so the power

---

*See John Maynard Keynes: *Essays in Persuasion*, New York, Harcourt Brace, 1932. part V.

age requires a certain social control but enlarges the
area of experimentation and adventure. The very
fact that business cannot operate unless everybody
spends his income means merely that the way is open
toward a great cultural advance. As soon as we stop
wasting our substance in riotous investment and unemployment, we can start spending it for those things that
make a great civilization: monumental buildings,
parks, recreation, education, religion, health, sport,
science, literature, drama, and all the arts of life. We
are the "primitives" of the great age now dawning.
We cannot plan its development. Destiny will work
through trials and false starts to something as far
beyond our dreams as the Parthenon was beyond the
dreams of the Argonauts. Our job is only to lay the
foundations.

The age of plenty, based on power, is only the material element of the new civilization. There will be
many other factors of mental attitude and social
organization, some of them already showing a definite
foreshadowing of their future growth. The technique
for using leisure time is only one example of the many
new fields into which human thought is expanding.
Most important of all, perhaps, is the reorientation of
our standards of value and of our judgments of right,
truth, and beauty.

It is not surprising that our minds are confused. For
half a million years mankind has struggled with the
problem of how to get plenty to eat without working
hard. There have been small local successes, in the
South Sea Islands, in Athens, in Renaissance Italy, in
Elizabethan England, each one flowering in a savage or
a civilized culture. But now for the first time the whole
Western world has broken through the age-old barrier.
Of course we are dazed. The moral virtues, the religion,

the philosophy of the old struggle have vanished. But already beneath the surface the intellectual and emotional foundations of the new order are being laid. Thrift is becoming avarice in our minds, extravagance becomes generosity or magnificence, the abolition of poverty seems more practical than its alleviation, the emphasis in religion begins to shift from its consolatory to its creative aspects,* philosophy begins to look toward new adventures.† The vanguard of human thought already breathes the air of the new world.

The old dream of a magic key to untold wealth has come true. We must have a new dream, and already it is forming. We dream of a world where lifelong fear, humiliation, and degradation will no longer be the common lot of the great mass of humanity. We dream of new arts and new adventures. How long or how painful may be the passage into our new civilization we cannot know. But all the signs point forward. The desert storm drives us on; ahead is the first glimpse of green hills and pleasant fields. The road of destiny is under our feet, and those who live through will see the promised land.

---

*See William Pepperell Montague, *Belief Unbound*, Yale Press, 1930.
†See Alfred North Whitehead: *Adventures of Ideas*, Macmillan Co., 1933.